TALKING
TO
LORD NEWBOROUGH

THE ALSOP REVIEW PRESS

For more information visit www.alsopreview.com

Design & Typography by Robt. Ward

ISBN 0-976-19541-0

Orders, enquiries, and correspondence should be addressed to:

Alsop Review, Ltd.
122 Broad Creek Road,
Laurel, DE 19956

TALKING
TO
LORD NEWBOROUGH

New & Selected Poems

· David Gwilym Anthony ·

THE ALSOP REVIEW PRESS

Acknowledgments

Some of these poems appeared in my first book, *"Words to Say"* (Pen Press Publishers, 2002, ISBN 1-904018-43-2) — and in the following books and magazines:

UK

Acumen
Candelabrum
Poetry Scotland
Snakeskin
The Sonnet at the Millennium *(Anthology)*
The Sun Also Rises
Worm
Write-away

USA

Anthology One *(Alsop Review Press)*
Artemis Journal
Avatar Review
Carnelian
Defenestration
Edge City Review
First Things
Light Quarterly
Mindfire Renewed
Octavo
Pierian Springs
The Susquehanna Quarterly
The Buckeye
The Eleventh Muse
The New Formalist
Writer's Hood

Japan

Contemporary Ten Thousand Leaves Anthology *(Gendai Manyo Shu)*
Eisuke Shiiki's Ran Pan Un
Tanka Journal

Dedication

For Brigid, with all my love

THE ALSOP REVIEW PRESS

Contents

People and Places

Talking to Lord Newborough 3
One-Way Ticket 4
Tale From a Gwynedd Village 5
Bloodlines 6
Jilted 7
Rameses II 8
To Gerard Manley Hopkins 9
Look Away 10
For The Beatles 11
Who'll Hold Their Hands? 12
On the Death of Princess Margaret... 13
And Her Mother 13
Tambourine Man 14
Flower Seller 15
Over America 16

Faith, Hope, and Occasional Charity

A Winter Funeral 19
Water Bearer 20
Flotsam on a Winter Tide 21
Summer's End 22
For All the Saints 23
Out of the Night 24
Knowing the Score 25

Friends and Family

Situation Vacant 28
Cushioning the Blow 29
To Die For 30
Who's Afraid? 31
On a Photograph of a Young Child 32
For My Daughter 33
I Thought You Were a Friend 34
Words to Say 35
On the Suicide of a Friend 36

Time and Seasons

Hawthorn 39

Warming 40

Five Views of Kyoto 41

Tallyman 42

Late August at Hadrian's Wall 43

Harry Potter 44

Remembered Wings 45

Plague 46

Crossing the Border 47

Older the Worse 48

Journeys

Passing Through the Woods 51

Navigator 52

The Road Taken 53

Concorde 54

Father of the Man 55

Running on Empty 56

In Search of Inspiration

Stuffing It In 59

Triolette 60

20/20 Vision 61

Slush Pile 62

Bird's Eye View 63

People and Places

Talking to Lord Newborough

I'd perch beside your gravestone years ago,
a boy who thought you old at forty-three.
I knew you loved this quiet place, like me.
We'd gaze towards Maentwrog far below,
kindred spirits, and I'd talk to you.
Sometimes I asked what it was like to die—
were you afraid? You never did reply,
and silence rested lightly on us two.

These days the past is nearer, so I came
to our remembered refuge on the hill,
expecting change yet finding little there:
my village and the Moelwyns look the same,
Saint Michael's Church commands the valley still—
but you, old friend, are younger than you were.

*(Lt. William Charles Wynn, 1873-1916, 4th Baron Newborough,
whose grave overlooks the Vale of Ffestiniog in North Wales)*

One-Way Ticket

They closed the line and just the track remains.
The miners' railway where we used to play
in far-off summers, when I came to stay,
echoes with the ghosts of long-gone trains.

Cwm Cynfal and the Ceunant ring with wild
unchanging songs of childhood. Years away
mean nothing there. When I returned today
they called to me, and knew me as their child.

The rest is altered irretrievably.
My kin died years ago or else moved on:
no point in staying once the work was gone.
How few there are who still remember me.

My ties are broken far beyond repair:
the line is closed and just the tracks are there.

(Cwm Cynfal and the Ceunant: the valley and gorge of the River Cynfal)

Tale From a Gwynedd Village

A cry cut through the winter's wind. "Who died?"
the student asked his mother, far away
in spirit from the friend he'd brought to stay.
"Poor Hywel Jones, God rest him", she replied.

The guest had heard of shadows that abide
in Celtic lands—those keening ghosts who stray
when souls are crossing—and he felt the fey
forebodings carried where the cold wind cried.

Across the road, a carpenter once more
bent to his task. The same old man who made
the babies' cots now fashioned with a sigh
a thing to hold no hope. His power saw
started to turn again. The cutting blade
bewailed an ending with its lonely cry.

Bloodlines

They're pictured wearing baubles carved from bone,
woad-daubed and fur-clad, flaunting tribal scars.
Such disrespect—such crude depiction—mars
the memories embedded in the stone
and in my blood, my every chromosome.
Why paint their culture worthless next to ours,
those men who traced the movement of the stars
and built Stonehenge before the birth of Rome?

Their mysteries live on within each cairn
and megalith, though little else remains:
like us they learned what pride and progress cost.
If we could call their spirits to return,
would they stand silent awed by all our gains—
or stricken seeing everything we've lost?

Jilted

So care no more, my love, for hope forlorn:
it leads us on and leads us all astray.
Let not the thought of noon obscure the dawn
and dim the brightness of the starting day;
or cheer your heart with prospects seeming fair,
or lift your soul before it starts to grieve
only to fling it deeper to despair.
Remember, hope's design is to deceive.

Bear your present grief: look not to some
vague hope to end your sorrowing, nor sigh
for better times to come. They may not come,
and hope will turn to anguish by and by.
Like you, dear, hope's a liar—if believed,
don't be surprised to find yourself deceived.

Rameses II

He's just a bag of bones, a wizened thing—
another curious object on display
for us to gawk at. This is not the way
to treat a traitor, let alone a king
who showed his people lofty places where
no other race had gazed or dared to go.
If death can bring so great a man so low,
what hope have we of any honour there?

Still, I have seen colossi raised beside
transcendent temples built to challenge time:
Egypt's apotheosis grave and wise
observes the generations. Ancient pride,
unfaded by the ages, bears his sign,
and shines reflected in his people's eyes.

(Known to the Greeks as Ozymandias; his mummy
is on display in Cairo Museum)

To Gerard Manley Hopkins

Your spirit hovered quivering, poised on air
of sense and sound, charged like a lightning rod:
now flashing out to seize the grace of God,
now plummeting in darkness and despair—
despair! Did wisdom really bring you there,
where tired generations trod and trod,
where feet convey no feeling, iron-shod,
where hopelessness hangs heavy everywhere?

Sometimes I wonder, did you understand
without the dark your candle could not glow?
Your soul was tortured by self-reprimand,
self-crucified, self-loathing; yet I know
the God you loved and hated took your hand
at last and led you safe where no storms blow.

Look Away

God-fearing Patriarch, you rose to smite
the North as Samson smote the Philistine:
the South's defender certain of divine
endorsement, confident your cause was right.
You whipped the Yankees squarely every fight
and championed your people's proud design,
till random bullets from the Rebel line
at Chancellorsville, foreshadowed Dixie's night.

Come, tired soldier, let us cross the stream
and rest beneath the shadow of a tree.
The centre fails; intruders reign supreme
and raze your land through Georgia to the sea.
The shadow deepens darkening a dream
as Dixie toils towards her Calvary.

("Let us cross over the river and rest under the shade of the trees":
last words of General Thomas "Stonewall" Jackson, May 1863)

For The Beatles

(on the death of George Harrison)

You showed us all, we all need love
and love is all. We need
your compass or we fear to move.
You showed us all, we all need love,
and how those simple songs can prove
abiding friends indeed—
you showed us all. We all need love,
and love is all we need.

Who'll Hold Their Hands?

Sometimes an image strikes a cruel blow:
I've seen deceit, behind a mask of care,
cut with a lash and lay the senses bare.
A bitter man's betraying kiss was so;
or those two youngsters caught on video—
ignored by passers-by (not their affair)—
who took a toddler's hand and led him where
there are dark truths we do not choose to know.

"Hanging's too good!" "They don't deserve to live!"
(But whose is the betrayal we recall?)
Did Christ, the friend to thief and fugitive,
greet Judas' kiss with empathy or gall?
They were our sins and so we can't forgive:
just ten years old. May God forgive us all.

(Jamie Bulger, aged two, was abducted and killed in Bootle,
Merseyside in 1993 by ten-year-old Jon Venables and Robert Thompson.)

On the Death of Princess Margaret...

(August 1930-February 2002)

The paparazzi came in force
and stole your daughter's grief.
You never owned your life, of course.
The paparazzi came in force
and plundered you without remorse,
but this defies belief:
the paparazzi came in force
and stole your daughter's grief.

And Her Mother

(August 1900-March 2002)

The sun that bravely shone at last went down.
Lie easy now, the head that wore a crown.

(Elizabeth the Queen Mother, last Empress of India)

Tambourine Man

(for Bob Dylan's 60th birthday)

His hair a thicket, voice a rasping saw
cutting through cant and conscience's decay—
my scruffy hero channelled youth's dismay
and changed the world in 1964.
His music called to me: I heard with awe
wild songs—they wheeled and soared above the day
then swooping drove indifference away.
Glad to be young I stood at heaven's door.

He calls again, and how could I resist
a ragged clown behind a reverie
still chasing wraiths within the day's grey mist?
It's darker now: I cannot sense or see
a way ahead but I can dance. Hey! Mist-
-er Tambourine Man, play a song for me.

Flower Seller

Glimpsed roses at a roadside stall: so bright
a contrast to the city's traffic haze,
rich with the peace and warmth of summer's days
and quiet reveries of dark and light;
seen only for a moment—there, then gone.
Such wistful beauty, such a brave display,
stands out against the drabness of the day,
confirming even here our dreams live on.

But wayside seller, looking at your face,
I see your flowers are only goods to sell
with no innate significance. Ah well,
there's little value in the commonplace.
Still I wonder, trapped within life's schemes
and compromises, did you sell your dreams?

Over America

(Jeremy Glick, United Airlines
Flight 93, 11 Sept. 2001)

A man spoke out from a lonely place
on his pocket telephone.
As he heard what end he would have to face
a man spoke out from a lonely place.
To bow to force could be no disgrace
yet he vowed to fight for his own.
A man spoke out for the human race
on his pocket telephone.

Faith, Hope, and Occasional Charity

A Winter Funeral

The church was cold in a sullen light
as we said goodbye to Ron.
Over the bier a moth took flight,
though the church was cold. In the sullen light
it fluttered down as a blessing might,
then gained the porch and was gone.
And the church was gold in a sudden light
as we said goodbye to Ron.

Water Bearer

Each dawn before the sun devoured the shade
and seared the arid land, a potter strode
down to the well along a dusty road
to fill a well-used water jar he'd made.

As he returned one day, a stranger said,
"Your jar is fractured. Anyone can see
you waste your time and labour fruitlessly.
The water spills along the track you tread."

The potter answered, "Though it leaks it still
retains enough for me, and I would not,
for all its flaws, discard my battered pot.
It has another purpose to fulfil."

Where he had passed, a radiant display
of flowers bobbed to greet the breaking day.

Flotsam on a Winter Tide

Round again on the full tide, churning
close to the quiet foreshore, then
caught by the undertow and turning
round again—

slowing now: as far-travelled men,
turning back with regret or yearning,
drift for a while near a journey's end.

Knowing all and beyond all knowing,
Nature speaks in the tide's turn, when
all that drifts is gathered, going
round again.

Summer's End

Yesterday,
stealing from the sun,
dandelions
lit the shaded path
briefly. Now they're gone.

Hurry through
faded meadows, while
light still holds.
Days grow shorter; how
quickly evening comes.

Stirred to rise
by a falling foot,
feathered seeds,
graceful on the breeze,
drift towards the dawn.

For All the Saints

For you brave martyr-saints, whose blood
refreshed the faith my fathers knew;
and you ascetic hermit-saints,
who lived where lonely wormwood grew;
and you remorseless soldier-saints,
who spread the Word with swords, and slew
wild unrepentant heathen hordes
in Jesus' name: I pray for you.
I pray your unrelenting cause
is not unworthy, or untrue.

Out of the Night

We saw your death—they showed it on TV—
and had revenge if vengeance was our goal.
You thanked the Gods, whatever Gods may be,
and spoke of your unconquerable soul.
We shared a God—no, not the one whose whole
existence was compassionate, who tried
by promising redemption to console
his wayward children, and was crucified.
We chose your sterner Deity as guide,
with ancient tribal precepts and a sword.
Though Hope and Charity did not abide,
Faith lived when our uncompromising Lord—
not often merciful but always just—
demanded eye for eye and dust for dust.

*(Timothy McVeigh, called the Oklahoma Bomber,
who chose Henley's "Invictus" as his epitaph)*

Knowing the Score

The slights I cherish sing to me
their old seductive song:
it's friends who always wound the worst—
the list I keep is long.
I don't much like the counterpoint,
a quiet voice but strong:
"Choose wisely when remembering;
love keeps no count of wrong."

(1 Corinthians 13)

Friends and Family

Situation Vacant

My cousins have a strong religious streak—
teetotal Bible belters. I don't like
those Jesus freaks: the worst one's Pastor Mike.
To my surprise I heard from him last week.
He wrote, "You've met my helper Pete, I think:
I used to take him with me when I went
to spread the Word. The man was heaven-sent
to demonstrate the ill effects of drink.
He'd drool beside me in the Gospel Hall
and urinate, then fall about the stage;
or, turning to my flock in drunken rage,
he'd stagger forth and vilify them all.
He's passed away, the poor pathetic slob:
so how about it—would you like the job?"

Cushioning the Blow

We thought it best to leave the cat with Ted
along with Grandma, when we went away.
No sooner were we home from holiday
than, bluntly, he announced the cat was dead.

"Listen!" I said, "Bad news is better told
obliquely—like this: 'Bess went climbing on
the roof, and fell. Her legs and back were gone.
They tried to save her but she was too old.' "

Ted—who's direct but not a thoughtless man—
was chastened (so he said) and mortified.
"Don't worry, Cousin Edward," I replied.
"We all drop clangers. By the way, how's Gran?"

"Not great," he said, "In fact, to tell the truth,
last night she went out climbing on the roof......"

To Die For

Aunt Bessie has a talent: when she bakes
the flavour drives you wild. My cousins say
their father Tim, a regular gourmet,
married her for love—of chocolate cakes.

Poor Uncle Tim was feeling far from well—
in fact, was on his deathbed—when the scent
of baking half-revived him. Off he went
to find the source of that seductive smell.

Each step was painful as he tottered down
to taste the treat. At last his feeble hand
grasped hungrily. Bess slapped it sharply and
dismissed him with an irritated frown:

"Clear off to bed and put the buns back too!
I made them for the funeral, not for you."

Who's Afraid?

My sister takes reception class and prides
herself on spinning yarns: at five years old
the kids when entertained are good as gold,
and learn a lot from fairy tales besides.
They loved the story of the pig who tries
to build a house of straw—the one the bold
and wicked wolf will wreck—a tale best told
in detail, showing all it signifies.

"The pig," she told them, "found a turnip bed
made out of straw and asked if he could dig
a little up. Guess what the farmer said?"
"I know," cried Jude, one hand above her head,
and standing (since she wasn't very big):
"Well, bugger me—here comes a talking pig!"

On a Photograph of a Young Child

Shining eyes and golden hair,
little soldier standing there—
may the future take you where
stars will always shine at night,
days will all be golden-bright.
May the touch of care be light.

For My Daughter

It's funny how I never saw you grow.
I seem to miss what's nearest as a rule,
far too preoccupied—a busy fool
blind to the way the seasons come and go.

What shall I give since now you're going too
and will be gone a while? Although you're brave
and self-assured, I know I rarely gave
a sign to show how proud I was of you.

I give it now, with love; but love's no gift:
it's yours by right. Because you're going far
I'll give a gentle light to be your star,
and all my hopes to hold when life's adrift.

I'll give them all, though all I have would be
no gift beside the gift you were to me.

I Thought You Were a Friend

(in memory of MJM)

I knew you well and thought you were a friend,
and yet you gave no sign you meant to go.
Is this the proper way for it to end?

The hardest thing for me to comprehend
was why you failed to say goodbye, although
I knew you well and thought you were a friend,

and never doubted once I could depend
on you. To my regret it was not so.
Is this the proper way—for it to end

so brusquely? I had always meant to spend
more time with you. It was a telling blow
from one I knew and thought of as a friend.

I would have stood beside you to defend
against the fear, though all I really know
is this: the proper way for it to end

is not the way the passing-bells pretend—
they ring with falsehood, sonorous and slow.
There was no proper way for it to end
for you who left me, though you were a friend.

Words to Say

The priest knew all the proper words to say.
He'd never met her but he had a note.
He mentioned everything her brother wrote
and said she'd had a good life anyway.

The old piano she would often play
still holds remembered cadences of those
Welsh melodies she loved, but I suppose
we'll sell it now since Betty's passed away.

I saw her schedules written on a chart
pinned to the study wall: she'd meant to speak
to Mum and booked the dentist for next week.
Strange, how the little things can break your heart.

I'd watched her growing weaker day by day,
but never found the proper words to say.

On the Suicide of a Friend

God help the kids! I heard the neighbours say—
so quick to judge though mostly they were kind.
They saw the sorry mess you left behind
and thought you took the coward's selfish way.

The coward's way? No, not that I can see.
Despair's a snare. They say a fox will gnaw
its fettered foot and sacrifice the paw.
What desperation drove you to break free?

Nor were you selfish. Just beneath the calm
the darkness gathered; I have known it too.
It touched those near. It's my conviction you
believed you were protecting them from harm.

God—if there's a God—will grant you rest:
you failed, we all do, but you did your best.

Time and Seasons

Hawthorn

Why are you weeping May Tree, May Tree,
why are you weeping May?
Springtime's fresh and the sun is high,
there is no blue like the morning sky
and winter's far away.
The season's glad so why be sad?
Why are you weeping May?

Why are you weeping May Tree, May Tree,
why are you weeping May—
shedding tears of perfect white,
pure as sorrow and white as light,
in garlanded decay?

Is it care for seasons yet to be?
Let's look away and refuse to see:
the year's young and so are we
and winter's far away.
Thoughts so cold never trouble me,
so cease your weeping May.
Please cease your weeping, May.

Warming

The seasons' course seems strange to me,
more strange than I remember;
wild flowers bloom unseasonably:
primroses in November.

The young pretend to blame us all.
Well, youth's a great dissembler:
May was forever I recall
and there was no November.

These days I'll take what Nature sends
to hoard for dour December:
a glow of warmth as autumn ends;
primroses in November.

Five Views of Kyoto

Gion bar—
homely, far from home.
We discuss
how to change the world
and the price of beer.

Geisha twins—
young or old, who knows?
Painted masks
safely cover old
passions, or young dreams.

I recline
graceless on tatami,
savouring
subtle food, while saké
soothes my gaijin's bones.

How they bend
to the blows of time!—
wooden shrines
ruined, rebuilt, unchanged:
fragile permanence.

Vestiges
of each age remain,
layered and
softly fading. Plum
blossom drifts on snow.

Tallyman

It seems no time since warmth replaced the cold,
and nature's careful plans were first displayed
in buds along the foxglove's stem, arrayed
profusely and preparing to unfold.

Tall tallyman, I know the price you pay:
your clustered blossoms nodding to the dawn
fade one for every evening as you mourn
the counted fall of every summer's day.

Too soon a wilder wind arriving, scours
the season's bright creations, stripping bare
the hedgerows and the woodland clearings where
you sacrifice your last and lonely flowers—

still beautiful, although the best are past,
and missed the most because they were the last.

Late August at Hadrian's Wall

April's spring
and October's fall:
both so loved—
one for promises;
one for memories.

Who could love
summer's sultry close?
Changes loom:
clouds, high-building, drift
nearer through the haze.

August though
bears a Caesar's name,
and the year,
stoic in decline,
stands, and holds a while.

Harry Potter

(for TK)

For all the years I still recall those rare
clairvoyant boyhood moments when my world
was new, and I glimpsed magic as it swirled
and scintillated in the morning air.

Grave young sorcerer you make me smile
with broomsticks, spells and potions. Every charm
defies the Dark Lord, shields your friends from harm
and conjures up my childhood for a while.

Time can't touch you. Even so, take care
to keep your youthful confidence and grace.
I will remember how your spirit shone
so bravely in the darkness of despair—
a talisman to ward us when we face
this grown-up world with all its magic gone.

Remembered Wings

Year after year their timing was the same.
As early summer took the place of spring
my swallows came, and briskly gathering
would breed then raise their young and so proclaim
hope's renaissance. Each darted sharp as flame
between the earth and sky, remembering
old haunts despite long miles of wandering.
This year I waited but they never came.

Autumn's a time for leaving: cherished things
are embers, as remembered flames burn low,
and vanish with the chill the first frost brings;
a time to grieve though now it isn't so:
never to greet those brave arriving wings
spares the pain of parting when they go.

Plague

The guns are loud across the land tonight.
Grim beacon flames flash out from shire to shire
and horror groans without an end in sight.

Best not to look as marksmen expedite
such slaughter. Hired to empty every byre,
the guns are loud. Across the land tonight

Spring flinches at the foulness of the blight
that lurks within the pall above each pyre,
and horror groans without an end, in sight

of pallid flames where all is darkly bright.
So draw the blinds and turn the music higher—
the guns are loud across the land tonight!

Send off the children. Let them still delight
in childish things; don't tell them life's a liar
and horror groans. Without an end in sight

there seems no point. Why carry on, why fight?
Not only cattle perish in the fire,
and horror groans without an end in sight.
The guns are loud across the land tonight.

(foot and mouth epidemic, spring 2001)

Crossing the Border

Fences are never needed: Herdwick sheep,
waking the Lakeland hills with wistful bleating,
have learned the boundaries they are to keep.
Fierce Viking settlers recognised the greeting
of each flock heafted to its native fell,
and cared for them through hardship, knowing well
how troubles pass and all revives with spring.
A harsher husbandry is now depleting
ancient herds, and old ways are retreating:
can thought forget the soul's remembering?
May we return some part of all we take,
and so reclaim the wisdom lost to man
to know our bounds; then nature shall remake
a truer borderline than fences can.

*(Herdwicks: a breed specific to the hills of Cumbria, with a
homing instinct known as "heafting" in Cumbrian dialect)*

Older the Worse

The swing of the seasons brings small cheer:
the world grows tired and groans,
and colours that once were crisp and clear
are faded to monochromes.
Fear prowls the night, and it lurks in light
as seed falls sterile on stones,
and spring struggles harder every year
to cover dread winter's bones.

Journeys

Passing Through the Woods

It's hard to see my way because
the leaves have fallen. Now
they're drifting where a path once was—
it's hard to see my way. Because
the light is brief I dare not pause;
I'll find the track somehow.
It's hard to see my way because
the leaves have fallen now.

Navigator

The drive engaged; electric sails unfurled,
then filled; I keyed a course, *h t t p://*
and started out across a cyber sea
in search of fellow feeling in the world.
I navigated oceans brightly pearled
with scattered islands of affinity
whose harbours sometimes seemed like home to me,
safe havens when despair and discord swirled.

Seafarers slightly known and swiftly gone,
some here to learn and all with things to say:
those strangers warming in the light that shone
from empathy, had little time to stay.
Minds met a moment, touched and travelled on
to look for something lost and far away.

The Road Taken

Youth's urgency permitted no delay
and many paths diverged. I didn't know
which one to take or where I ought to go,
and settled for a broad and trodden way
because it offered light and company;
but as my friends dispersed along the road
I travelled on alone, and often strode
in haste where I had no desire to be.

At evening everything becomes opaque,
and circumstance has turned the track I chose
back on itself, much nearer now to those
remembered byways I shall never take.
This is a light to me when dark is near:
the paths diverged but all at last led here.

Concorde

March 1969—October 2003

Her spring was in the heady era when
we landed on the moon—*One giant leap*
directed at the stars. Though we may keep
our dreams, it seems we will not go again.

I used to pause to watch her passing by,
and she was beautiful: not just a plane,
an aspiration soaring to reclaim
the wonder of an ancient urge to fly.

Now she's gone as well. Once steadfast, we
set out to sever every bond of land,
to challenge space, but stalled. I understand:
the world is tired, growing old like me,
and aspiration fails. They look so steep,
those heights our giants once resolved to leap.

Father of the Man

Daunted by the shadows in my mind,
uncertain where the hazy pathways led
and frightened by the darkness up ahead,
I saw my Youth approaching from behind
and paused and waited, thinking what to say.
We'd broken contact many years ago—
we hadn't much in common. Even so
his certainty might help me find the way.

He came to meet me coldly with a frown,
and I fell silent, angered, filled with such
resentment that this parent asked so much,
but sadness too because I'd let him down.

So burdened by the weight of wasted days
we drew apart and went our different ways.

Running on Empty

Preoccupied, I overtook the years
and never saw the moments racing by.
The future seemed worth chasing then and I,
knowing how expectations outrun fears,
was restless, restless—unprepared to wait
or turn to where the present was. The pain
of losing things I'd never see again
was nothing; but it troubles me of late.

Time modifies perception. Even though
what does remain is altered, and ahead
are lonely roads where apprehensions spread,
I will not fear to go where shadows grow—
still restless though anticipation's gone.
The gauge reads empty but the wheels roll on.

In Search of Inspiration

Stuffing It In

Today I feel the urge to do a sonnet:
I'll see to it before the morning's out.
Just one word rhymes with sonnet, but no doubt
a slant can be insinuated—Done it!
So far so good. Enjambment helps: let's run it
between the lines. I'm half-inclined to flout
the rule insisting on a turn, about
line nine. Screw Petrarch's horse! Who'd ride in on it?
But like the nag I'm knackered, so let's try
to reach a lazy climax; soon be there:
just ease it in, far better not to force it.
Sonnets are like those garments ladies buy—
I'm thinking of restraining underwear.
Sometimes the bulges overcome the corset.

Triolette

I think I'll write a triolet—
but does it rhyme with get or gay?
I'm ignorant I know, and yet
I think I'll write a triolet,
and make a rhyme with gay, or get—
who gives a toss whichever way?
I think I'll write a triolet—
but does it rhyme with get or gay?

20/20 Vision

Some tell me my stuff is myopic,
or (crueller still) amblyopic.
I find consolation
in Clive's observation:
as clear as the day it's diplopic.

> *"I cannot decide whether [your] diplopia works in the*
> *sense of adding emotional and mythic resonance…"*
> —*Clive Watkins, Eratosphere*

Slush Pile

In some respects I like this, even though
the workmanship's not great. Who'd rhyme 'today'
with 'day'? This one's arcane: what does it *say*?
Two down now; just two hundred more to go.
Call that a poem? Prose! And this is so
Poetic. Why must people disobey
the basic rules of syntax? No. No way,
and No, and No, and No, and No, and No,

and......Oh. Here's something special: see it shine.
It coruscates: a lantern made of gold
revealing vistas formerly unseen.
I sense the presence of a noble soul
who dares to go where others have not been.
Ah, now I recollect: it's one of mine!

Bird's Eye View

As if I work for him—how could he know
the weight of all my cares?—a robin hops
towards me from the border; then he stops
to watch me push my mower to and fro.
He looks for worms along the fresh-cut line,
while I seek inspiration for a gem
to stun my critics—how I'll dazzle them!
The bird has his agenda; I have mine.

My chore complete, I settle down to wring
some essence from our interaction. Now
a sharp deflating insight has unfurled
its wings. (I *had* been contemplating how
absurd it was for such a little thing
to think himself the centre of the world.)

David Gwilym Anthony was born in Ffestiniog, Gwynedd, North Wales, and soon afterwards his family moved to Hull. He was educated at Hull Grammar School and St Catherine's College, Oxford, where he studied modern history. He writes:

"My life's been spent in the near aura of famous poets: Dafydd ap Gwilym, greatest of the Welsh bards; Philip Larkin, one-time librarian of Hull University; Andrew Marvell, another old boy of Hull Grammar School. I live now with my family in Stoke Poges, Buckinghamshire, a stone's throw from the churchyard where Thomas Gray is buried, still hoping one day something of these poets will rub off on me.

I regarded poetry as a solitary pursuit, till I discovered the internet a few years ago. I now have many poetry friends in the virtual world. I'm more than grateful for their invaluable suggestions, and their enormous contribution to this book."

David works in London, in financial services.

You can contact him at http://www.davidgwilymanthony.co.uk

Dr. Merfyn C Davies, illustrator, was also born in Ffestiniog, where his father (David's grandfather) was the village carpenter and builder. Like David, Merfyn moved away when young. Unlike David, he is a native Welsh speaker.

Before retirement he taught architecture at Nottingham University.

www.ingramcontent.com/pod-product-compliance
Lightning Source LLC
LaVergne TN
LVHW091207080426
835509LV00006B/882